THE BLACK SUNFLOWER

Dezz

Copyright © August 2021, Destiny Nicholson
Wider Perspectives Publishing, Norfolk, Va
ISBN: 978-1-952773-37-2

Acknowledgment

To my sisters,
I wouldn't have been able to grow if
I didn't watch you do it first.

Contents

Root

Stem

Fallen Leaves

Thriving Petals

ROOT

The Hood

"I made up my mind,
No, I'm not losing to these streets.
In fact
I won't be going back until they name one after me."

When you're from the hood...

People will look at you one of three ways.
1. In disgust.
    They've never seen the scum between their toes up
    close
2. In fear.
    They immediately assume you lie, steal and cheat.
    Have a habit of making a scene
3. In pity.
    Maybe they're from there.
    Know what it's like there.
    Know how hard it is to make it out of there.

Or maybe they've come up with ideas in their head,
About how hard your life has to be.

They'll assume you have zip code envy
The west side is only the best side
For the purpose of a rap song.

Where I'm from girls like to wear short skirts,
Boys wear guns to compliment their white beaters.
Big words are often mistaken for fighting words,
Only when they make her feel inferior
When we need healing we go to our grandmothers.
Our grandmas pray harder than police bodyslam us on
the streets.

It matters what colors you're wearin'
Can't be accidentally reppin'
Teachers stopped caring
Or maybe they never started

We were never problem children.
Just children dealing with adult problems

He, at age, 15 had two jobs
Just so they could make ends meet
So he was tired
Would fall asleep during class.
No one took the time to understand

She had 3 younger siblings, a single mother
who wasn't healthy
If you know what I mean
She took on full responsibility of guarding their innocence

We grow up quick, fast, and in a hurry
Experience more trauma than the world cares to admit
They won't call it PTSD
We ain't worth the label
Just have to suck it up

That I've seen friends die
Fireworks sound like gunshots
I don't like the fourth of July
A text reassuring you got home safe is vital

If you die...
They'll tell the world what you were doing
Selling drugs, stealing, smoking weed

Nobody will tell the world why
They never taught us how to live
Only how to survive

To them we ain't even worth the sidewalk memorials
our mothers will leave.
They'd rather cage us
Than educate us
But I,

"I made up my mind,
No, I'm not losing to these streets.
In fact I won't be coming back
Unless they name one after me"

My Momma

Growing up as one of the only black kids in my school
Often the only one in my class
Often the only one in my grade
Yo momma jokes when directed at me often went
something like this,
"Yo momma is so black...."

Let me tell y'all about my momma

My momma is so black
That there is a capital letter in the middle of my
middle name
It is spelled L, a, capital R, e, e

My momma is so black
she smells like cocoa butter.
Got skin soft like velvet,
Dimples deep like the ocean

My momma is so black
The wig she wears
Depends on the way she feels

My momma is so black she will try every natural
home remedy in the book
Before prescription medicine
I'm talking chicken noodle and Vix VapoRub on deck

My momma is so black
Her middle name
Is Lavern

My momma is so black
I'm probably gonna get my ass beat for telling y'all her
middle name is Lavern

My momma is so black

That when she works 11 hour shifts
She calls it a short day
Says she was taking it easy

My momma is so black
That she never let us know when she was struggling
always did what she thought was best for us

My momma is so black
That she continues to heal
From generational curses
So that we, her children, can heal

My momma is so black
That she prays for all 6 of her children regularly
When not all 6 of her children can even call her,
regularly
She prays for us because in her eyes
Everytime we leave our houses we are risking our lives

My momma is so black
That she's loved me even when I didn't deserve it
While I was mad at her for simply being human
She was praying to God for my health

My momma is so black
That she doesn't say God, she says Gawd
Her Gawd is an awesome God
Her Gawd is a faithful God
God listens when she call

Hell, God better listen when my momma calls

My problem with God
Is that he has the audacity to let my mother hurt
While he might never give her something she can't handle
He often gives her things I can't always handle
watching her go through

My momma has been going through hell
but would still help someone if they need it
I've seen her cross oceans for people
Who wouldn't jump over puddles for her
Just because they needed it
Not for a second ever regrets it

My momma is so black!
My momma is so black!
My momma is so black!

She makes me want to stand in the sun a little longer
At the end of the day
I'm just tryna be like her

Daddy's Girl

My dad has three daughters
One biologically
Two that don't share an ounce of his DNA
If you ask, he'll tell you he has three.
Feeling no need to explain

I remember
I was 12
When I first called him daddy
I was 12 the first time I saw my daddy cry
He's always given me the best advice
Like "Don't let anyone tell you that I am not your dad"

I remember
Becoming obsessed with puzzles,
Confiding in my dad that every piece had a place
It all just made sense, unlike life

His reply, "The pieces don't know they have a place
until you put them there."
Going out and buying me more puzzles

I remember
Daddy daughter dates
My sisters always had to come along
But it never felt any less special

I remember
My sister trying to teach him how to do my hair

I remember
The first time we talked about boys

I remember
Beating him in air hockey
Falling asleep in his back seat
Him buying me my favorite snacks just because
Helping me with math
How to tell time
Every gem he's ever given me

I remember him loving me
Even when I was too young to realize that's what
he was doing
Even when I felt like I didn't deserve it

My dad is a superhero
Always had the strength to pour life into me and my
sisters even when he was falling apart
He saved us before we even knew we were in danger

They say, "A girl will end up with a guy that is
just like her dad."
And to that I say, "I pray I'm that lucky."

I may not share an ounce of his DNA
But his love, his love is what made me
No one in this world can tell me that is not my daddy.

Grandma's Hands

We used to go to church every Sunday.
Grandma sitting in the front row
With her giant church hat on and her fan

Next to her, her purse
Which had all the strawberry candies and
butterscotch
Needed to keep us kids quiet

This woman has been singing longer than I've been speaking
Praying longer than I've been breathing
In her hands you will find healing

My grandma is the definition of a back bone
Was generous enough to pass it down
Gave it to my mother
Who gave it to me
I will give to my children
Telling them stories of my grandma

Who has seen things she never speaks of
Who has more strength than meets the eye
Who has experienced more pain than you can imagine
Who smiles so wide when she sees her grandchildren

I hope she knows
She taught me, believing is half the battle
The importance of family

There's a piece of her in everything I do
I have memories of backyard barbeques
And her banana pudding

I hope she knows I would not be who I am
If it weren't for my grandma's hands

My Son

A friend of mine has this poem
For the life of me, I can't remember the title of it.

I remember the first line tho
The way he stands up tall,
Shoulders back,
Fingers in the air and says
"I kiss my son."

He doesn't say it like it's a confession
No hint of apology
A statement
A point-blank, period.

We spend so much time trying to protect our daughters
While letting our sons fend for themselves
Like they don't need protection

Like they don't have feelings
Like they don't cry
Like they don't need to be uplifted

Like only our daughters can be flowers

He was raised to be unlike the men in my life
Who left when things got too hard
Ran to the bottle.
Used their fists to show their love

He was raised to be better
He is better

You may think it's cute
To tell your friends how some little boy came to pick
your daughter up
And you answered the door with your gun

You threatened him
Out of fear that he would mistreat her

Not Knowing
He was raised with act right in his veins
Love in his heart
Communication skills beyond his years
You see he comes from a mother fuckin' poet

He understands while guns can end lives
Words can start revolutions

I don't know what made you think that
Pulling a gun on my son
Would make him scared of you

Momma raised a lot of things
But she ain't raised any of her children
To fear toxic masculinity
He fears one thing for certain
That's me when I'm angry

Now you might think I'm mad
I'm not.
I'm scared
That's my baby
While I'm raising him to be a King
People will still view him as the enemy
Will still reach for their weapon
Before even asking his name

You see I kiss my son.
Point, blank, period.
He will be a better man for it

But first,
The world has to give him the chance to live

Child-ish

We were kids
Back when
A kid being a kid was in

We watched rugrats on an orange cassette tape,
Made mud pies
Did the real harlem shake

Saturday morning cartoons
Started at 6 and ended at noon

We'd put a playing card on the wheel of our bikes
To seem cool
We'd create hammocks by tying sheets to the rails of
our bunk beds

Pretended mole hills were mountains
That we were unstoppable
The only thing we were scared of was the belt

Do you remember?

I understand we did it faster than others
Our environment forced us to grow up
But it bothers me
You see

Went from playing hopscotch
Eating pop rocks
Now it's gunshots
That won't stop

And you're mad at me for leaving

Remember we used to be super heros?
Saying when we were big enough we would protect her
Make him stop hitting her

Remember, you were supposed to be a doctor
Me; the red power ranger
Saving people,
I'd protect and defend While you tend to the wounded

What happened?
You see, The man standing in front of me
Is nowhere near who that little boy wanted to be

Keep saying you're mad at me for leaving
But if you were as serious as I was about being a
superhero
Then you should know

The first people we were supposed to save were
ourselves

STEM

Record

Singing the words of my song
Never acting

Preaching,
Never practicing

Hearing,
Never listening

Saying you want change,
Never changing

Muted my song,
Then have the audacity to ask why I'm not singing

Fuck Boy

You be on that fuck boy shit!
On that I wouldn't know honesty if it hit me like a
truck boy shit

That I don't want you, but no one else can have you
When I see you with a new dude is when I'll decide
to text you
"Very cute" with an attitude

Man, I swear you be on that fuck boy shit!

That I won't tell you you're beautiful
Yet get mad when some other dude does

That I don't want a relationship,
But I don't exactly not want a relationship
Like that makes any sense

I think you forgot who I is,
But look who it is
Always on time with it
That 2 A.M. "you up" text
Like the world don't know my bedtime is 10:30

Like I don't Know the only reason you texted me
Is because she didn't answer
Tryna feed me bullshit sprinkled with game on it
Expecting me to Know no better

I however,
Am not her,
I don't put just anything into my body.

You see you be on some fuck boy shit!
Can't even publicly acknowledge me
Guess your new toy is distracting

He's like, "Baby don't be that way."
First of all don't call me baby.
Second of all
You be on that fuck boy shit!

You can go out and be with whoever you want
When I do so it's a problem

That shit is for the birds
I guess that's why you always tweetin'
Not practicing what you preachin'

Do what I say, not as I do, but I'm not your children
You need to chill man

Last time I checked your favorite line was,
"We not together, tho."
You can stay on that fuck boy shit
I have more important things to handle

We can call it "grown woman shit"
My "momma raised me better than this" shit
My "I know my worth" shit
Hell, call me main character
This is the matrix
You can miss me with that bullshit.

I Am Not a Snack

He said, "Damn, you're thick."
I replied with an, "OK"
So he reassured me it was a compliment

"When did your ass get so fat?"
Referring to me as a whole snack

The thing about snacks
At least the ones in my house
They only last about a week
If they are around longer it's because
I forgot they were there
I keep them around to give me a fix
something quick
Or when I'm just too lazy to put in the time and effort
that comes with a full meal

They don't fill you up, They sustain you
A few hours after that snack,
You forget what you even had
Go out and get another one

They said, "You wore those heels for us, to give us something to look at."
I wore these heels so I could see over that big ego you got

He said, "I'm taking that home tonight."
Me remaining lady-iike said, "Who the fuck are you calling a that?"

I am not a "that"
I don't want to be your snack

You see me, I want to be somebody's full meal
I want to give you what you want as well as what you need
I would like you to see the nutritional value about me

When God was creating me he was not shy about the spices or seasoning
Ensuring I taste as good on the cold dark of winters
As I do on the warm days of summer

Saying to himself, 'When someone gets a taste of my creation,
They're gonna be like,
"Man God is good.
He knew exactly what he was doing,
When he was doing it
God really put his foot in this."'

So no, you will not be taking me home
If you're gonna come to me
You need to come correct

I am not a vending machine,
You will have to give me more than pennies
If you expect to get something out of me
Please excuse me
These heels are starting to hurt my feet

His Shot

He shot his shot

Refusing to believe his ball and my basket don't mix

Someone told him persistence is key

Someone taught him applying pressure get results

Now I can't walk without stepping on bullet casings
My shoes are double knotted
For I know he's gonna keep shooting
So I'm prepared to run

If, by chance, he hits me
As the blood leaves my body
I already know what they'll be saying,
"Boys were just being boys."

Giving him permission to find another target
Giving him permission to continue to shoot

You Want Me To Apologize

You want me to apologize
For my seductive brown eyes
My thick thighs

For showing you what my stomach looks like
They say I show too much belly out for the world to see

You want me to apologize
After all I was asking for it
Hand out begging for it
Knew what that dress would do when I wore it
Slit too high for me to think any different

You want me to apologize
Because boys were just being boys the way we taught them
While I was out "acting grown", "being fast"
I provoked him
The beast is what I awoke in him
The strength in me is what I had to dig for
When I was positive I couldn't fight any more

And you want me to apologize
For fighting
For running
For making him bleed

He thinks how a lot of you think
That no means maybe
No means try harder
No means pin me down so I don't move
Cover my mouth so they don't hear me scream
No means you're gonna give it to me anyway

You want me to apologize
After all I was asking for it
Hand out begging for it
Knew what that dress would do when I wore it
That crop top
Those jeans
Those sweats
That oversized t-shirt
That hoodie
I knew exactly what that hoodie would do when I wore it

You want me to apologize
After all I know better than to be
A woman, young lady, a little girl
Having the audacity to walk down the street
What the fuck has gotten into me

They turned me breathing into me asking for it
Said I had my hands out begging for it

And I knew exactly how they'd paint the picture once
I told them about it

Why should I have to apologize
I'm tired of having to apologize
When all I was trying to do was walk down
the Goddamn street
My apology

The Race

I spent most of my life trying to be someone else
Black girl held magic
Used the white man's science to minimize it

Not Knowing
They have no understanding of our power
They can not contain all of the light attached
to our spirits
Can not sell our authenticity to the highest bidder

Wearing our hair styles will not give them our grace
Our clothes will not give them our strength

But 10 year old me did not Know this
She Knew the hot comb and perm box better
than the scriptures
Spoken by grandmother

Understood her Kinky coils made her undesirable
Practiced her big words
"They will not call us ignorant."

She just wanted to be a part of the race
Not Knowing they change the rules every time we're
about to win

FALLEN

LEAVES

Fire

We were dancing with flames
As if the motion of our bodies
Somehow diluted the smell of danger
It was beautiful

43

Tree House (Bridges)

My brother Bridges had this treehouse
That someone felt the need to disassemble
Claiming their sledge hammer was love

I know exactly how it feels to have your safe place
ripped away from you
Tainted
By people who never saw the safeness in it

I've felt the anger that comes along with the heartbreak
I've panicked because all of a sudden I wasn't safe
anymore

My heart found refuge in the bottom of my stomach
As my words found refuge in the back of my throat.

I wanted to scream, "Fix it! Fix it! You broke it, now
fucking fix it."

You broke the place I viewed as home
When your arms told me
I couldn't live there anymore

Picture

A picture is worth a thousand words

There are pictures of us still tucked away in my drawer
Did they become silent?
Do they have nothing left to say?
Have they reached their thousand word limits?

What of all the words that went left unspoken?
I thought we were picture perfect
While you found your perfect picture to be the one that
I am not in

Song

I used to say
I want a love so intense
They write songs about it

Until I realized it meant
When it's over
People will be dancing on the ashes
Of my happiness

Scar

You didn't just push me away
You let go
Watched me fall into the stampede
Something straight out of the Lion King

And it killed me

Truth

Some people rather fall apart than face the truth
Truth is, with her you have a smile I've never seen before

I bet you write her love letters
Engrave all the reasons she's the best thing to happen
to you onto paper

I bet you play guitar when neither one of you can sleep
I bet she sings
Or dances as your fingers do upon the strings

In everyone of those stolen glances
I bet you fall deeper and deeper in love

I bet you've written songs about her that only your
piano knows

And I'll bet your pen has forgotten my name

THRIVING

PETALS

Dear Sunflower

Dear sunflower in the rose garden,
You are different
It doesn't matter how many times you try to stain your
petals red
You were never designed to be a rose

You are crafted with purpose in every one of your petals
Stem so strong you don't need to grow thorns in order
to protect your peace
Some see luck
I see strength
As you continue to reach for the sun, for the light in
the dark places

Some shrivel up under the heat
While you look it dead in the face
And scream, "This is what made me."

The sun has never dared dim its light for anybody
I hope you never dim yours
Shine
Grow
Rise

The reason you never belonged in a rose garden
Is because you were always meant to outgrow them

Art

We are what walking art looks like

Some see us "Painted by Van Gogh"
Others see us as "Graffitti"

We took the thousand word limit given to pictures
And exceeded it
Decided we have more to say

We speak pain
Truth so ugly it's damn near beautiful

Yet some people have a problem
View us like we need to be cleaned
View us as if we are not visual representation of
where we come from

We are what walking art looks like

Some see us as "Painted by Van Gogh"
Others see us as "Graffitti"

We are still art
Even if they don't understand the concept

Ink Stains

I have ink stained fingertips
From all the times I wanted to cry, but couldn't
From all the times I laughed, and no sound came out
From every time the Mentos of emotions dropped
into my Coke bottle body

I wrote a poem about it
When I was 5, and you were mean
My first time on stage
Dancing in the street
The friends that grew with me
As well as the ones who didn't

I wrote a poem about it
Our first kiss
That peaceful day on the beach
Trusting again
When our fire kept me warm
As well as when it burned me

My ink stained finger tips reminds me I'm alive
Reminds me to stand in my truth
Reminds me to live in the now
Reminds me to breathe

Concrete

Not all roses started in pots on someone's windowsill
Some of us had to brave the wild from birth
Had to fight for a spot in a garden that never saw
us as flowers

Ask us how we survived
We'll say, "We had to become stronger than the concrete
used to bury us."

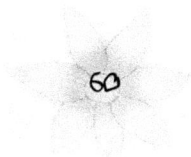

I Apologize

I apologize
For every time I made you feel less than you are
Like you weren't enough, You are more than enough

For every fight where I had to make you feel small in
order to win
For every negative thought that I put in you head
For not love you like an unfinished painting
Meeting you right where you are
Telling you that you are beautiful and will only get
better from here

This is my apology.....to me
Because honestly you deserved better

Black Sunflower

We lay connection to Apollo
Greek god associated with music, art, poetry and healing
As powerful and bright as the sun itself

They call us sunflowers
For we are always searching for the sunshine
We hold the sun's rays in our skin
Our hair stands on ends
As it tries to reunite with the light

They will say
That black sunflowers don't exist

I've seen them
Growing in circumstances that have caused others to shrivel
Walked beside them
As they found their place in the world
Laughed with them
Loved with them
Grew
In a field of them

<u>colophon</u>

Brought to you by Wider Perspectives Publishing, care of J. Scott Wilson, with the mission of advancing the poetry and creative community of Hampton Roads, Virginia.
See our production of works from ...

Edith Blake
Tanya Cunningham-Jones
Taz Weysweete'
Terra Leigh
Ray Simmons
Samantha Borders-Shoemaker
Bobby K.

J. Scott Wilson (TEECH!)
Charles Wilson
Gloria Darlene Mann
Neil Spirtas
Zach Crowe
Jorge Mendez & JT Williams
Sarah Eileen Williams
Stephanie Diana (Noftz)
the Hampton Roads

Jason Brown (Drk Mtr)
Martina Champion
Tony Broadway
Ken Sutton
Crickyt J. Expression
Lisa M. Kendrick
Cassandra IsFree
Nich (Nicholis Williams)
Samantha Geovjian Clarke
Natalie Morison-Uzzle
Gus Woodward II
Patsy Bickerstaff
Catherine TL Hodges
Jack Cassada
Chichi Iwuorie

... and others to come soon.

We promote and support the artists of the 757
from the seats, from the stands,
from the snapping fingers and
clapping hands
from the pages, and the stages
and now we pass them forth
to the ages

Check for the above artists on FaceBook, the Virginia Poetry Online channel on YouTube, and other social media.

Hampton Roads Artistic Collective is charitable extension of WPP which strives to simultaneously support worthy causes in Hampton Roads and the local creative artists.

www.ingramcontent.com/pod-product-compliance
Lightning Source LLC
Chambersburg PA
CBHW051708090426
42736CB00013B/2595